WHEN GOD SAYS NO, EAT *Cake*

FINDING COMFORT IN GOD DESPITE SETBACKS IN LIFE

RHONDA ❖ VELEZ

ISBN: 978-1-966798-33-0

Has God ever said *no* to something you deeply desired? Have you found yourself wrestling with disappointment, questioning His plan, or struggling to trust His timing? You're not alone.

When God Says No: Eat Cake is more than just a book—it's an invitation to shift your perspective, find peace in the waiting, and embrace joy even when life doesn't go as planned.

Join the journey. Dive into these pages and discover how to navigate God's "no" with faith, grace, and even celebration.

Reflect and grow. Use the reflection questions at the end of each chapter to process your own story and deepen your trust in God.

Embrace the sweetness. Instead of striving for control, what if you surrendered, trusted, and even *celebrated* God's perfect plan? Sometimes, the best response to a closed door is faith... and maybe even cake.

Are you ready to trust God's *no* and discover the unexpected goodness on the other side? Let's walk this journey together. Grab your copy today and take the first step toward peace, surrender, and joy.

The Marked Moment of Eating Cake

That moment marked the beginning of a deep and painful yet beautiful transformation. I had spent so much of my life striving, working hard, praying hard, believing that my effort and faith would bring the outcome I wanted. But what happens when God says *no*? What do we do when the doors we desperately want to walk through remain shut?

Maybe you've been there. Maybe you're there right now. You've prayed for healing, for a relationship to be restored, for that long-awaited opportunity. You've done everything "right," and still, the answer is silence or an unmistakable *no*. It's in these moments that our faith is truly tested—not in whether we can keep believing for the outcome we desire, but in whether we can trust that God is still good, even when things don't go our way.

This book is an invitation to see God's *no* through a different lens—not as rejection, but as redirection. Not as punishment, but as protection. Not as the end of the story, but as a divine setup for something better, even if we can't see it yet.

And sometimes, the best way to embrace that truth is to stop striving, surrender the outcome to God, and yes... eat cake.

So, if you've ever wrestled with disappointment, questioned God's plan, or wondered why He didn't answer the way you hoped, you're not alone. Let's walk this journey together, finding joy, trust, and maybe even a little bit of sweetness along the way.

Because sometimes, when God says no, it's time to stop fasting and start celebrating.

Let's dig in.

Table of Contents

Dedication

To my family—Jason, Nina, and Kalia—you have been my greatest supporters, my first audience, and my sounding board through every step of this journey. We have walked through so many "no's" together, faced heartbreak, wrestled with the hard conversations, and pushed through the days when giving up felt easier. Yet, through it all, we've held onto faith, hope, and each other.

Our story is uniquely ours, yet I know so many will see pieces of their own journey in these devotionals. Thank you for your love, your patience, and your unwavering belief in me. And to my angel in heaven, Tiana—you are the heartbeat of this book, the inspiration behind every word. I carry you with me always.

I love you all more than words can say.

Introduction:
Embracing the Unexpected "No"

I have a deep appreciation for meaningful devotionals. There's something truly special about their short stories and insights that provide moments for reflection and inspiration. As I pondered a title for this devotional, I realized that I've faced many times in my life when it felt like God was saying "No." Initially, these moments felt like rejection or punishment, but as I look back, I see that God's "No" was often a redirection toward something greater for my ultimate good.

Let's be honest—hearing "No" or "Wait" from God can stir up a storm of emotions. Fear, anger, and sadness often rise to the surface when our plans are disrupted and we're steered away from the paths we had hoped to take. This devotional is about exploring those feelings and understanding why God's redirection, though difficult, is always for our benefit.

The Bible offers us comfort and insight during these times. Proverbs 19:21 reminds us, "Many are the plans in a person's heart, but it is the Lord's purpose that prevails." When God says "No," it's not a denial of our desires but a way to align us with His perfect plan.

As we embark on this journey together, I encourage you to:

- Be open to receiving God's messages, even when they challenge your expectations.
- Embrace moments of stillness to listen intently to what God is communicating.
- Allow yourself to be vulnerable and honest about the emotions that arise when facing His redirection.

So, are you ready to dive in? Grab your favorite cup of tea or coffee—don't forget the cake—and find a cozy spot. Let's embark on this transformative journey together, discovering the sweetness that can be found even in life's unexpected "No."

Day 1

Plan your Exit

Habakkuk 3:17-19

"When God says no, eat cake" might sound quirky, but it's a heartfelt reminder to find joy and solace in life's little pleasures, even when things don't go as planned. It's about embracing the sweetness of life's simple joys, like savoring a piece of cake, even when you're facing setbacks or disappointments. When doors close or plans falter, let yourself enjoy these small, delightful moments—they can be a balm for your soul.

Habakkuk 3:17-19 paints a vivid picture of holding onto joy amidst adversity: "Even though the fig trees have no blossoms, and there are no grapes on the vines; even though the olive crop fails, and the fields lie empty and barren; even though the flocks die in the fields, and the cattle barns are empty, yet I will rejoice in the Lord! I will be joyful in the God of my salvation! The Sovereign Lord is my strength! He makes me as surefooted as a deer, able to tread upon the heights."

The other morning, I was jolted awake by the blaring alarm. As I reached over to silence it, my phone buzzed with a notification—an email from work. Normally, I'd glance at it quickly, but this one stopped me in my tracks. No contract renewal for our division in 2025. Was I about to be laid off? My heart raced as I texted my team for clarification. Their response confirmed my worst fears.

Still in my pajamas, I felt a strange mix of relief and anxiety. I had been unhappy at work, but leaving behind the familiar was daunting. I'd been praying for guidance and felt a nudge to wait until July. Now, with an 11 am meeting with HR and my manager on the horizon, the reality of my situation was sinking in.

As I rushed to drop off my car for service, the weight of the impending conversation felt heavy. Back at home, I took a deep breath and joined the call. Opening my notepad, I noticed a note from months ago: "PLAN YOUR EXIT." The irony wasn't lost on me. The call was brief, but its impact was profound. Tears threatened as questions swirled in my mind. Why now, God? With wedding expenses and car troubles adding to the uncertainty, I felt overwhelmed.

Amid this chaos, I turned to scripture for comfort. Jeremiah 17:7 says, "Blessed is the one who trusts in the Lord, whose confidence is in him." Trusting Him wasn't easy, but it was essential. As I navigated this challenging moment, I reminded myself that God's provision and timing are perfect, even when they're hard to see.

Reflection Questions:

1. How did you balance the feelings of relief and anxiety upon receiving unexpected news?
2. In what ways did this experience shift your understanding of God's timing and provision?
3. How can you cultivate a deeper trust in God's plan, even when facing uncertainty?

Conclusion:

Even when life feels like it's falling apart and you're hit with disappointment, remember to find joy in the small things that bring sweetness to your days. Just as Habakkuk rejoiced in the Lord despite his circumstances, you can hold onto hope and trust in God's provision. Embrace the little moments of joy, and let them remind you of His unchanging love and faithfulness.

Day 2

Finding Refuge in the Storm

Psalm 16:1 says, *"Keep me safe, O God, for in you I take refuge."*

This verse feels like a lifeline, especially after a particularly rough day. It's a gentle reminder that when life feels like it's falling apart, God is our safe harbor. Recently, I had one of those days where everything seemed to spiral out of control.

With my job hanging in the balance until June 5th, each call and message felt like an additional weight on my shoulders. Then there was that job interview I had pinned my hopes on. But when the call came, it wasn't the news I had hoped for. Rejection hit me hard, and it felt like I was drowning in a sea of disappointment.

Sitting outside with tears streaming down my face, I felt lost in a storm. Just when I thought it couldn't get worse, my phone blared with a tornado warning. In the midst of the chaos, I found a sliver of clarity. I realized how precious and fragile life is, and how much I needed to hold on to something solid amidst the whirlwind.

Questions flooded my mind. What was God's plan in all this? How was I supposed to navigate this uncertainty? It felt like being caught in a tornado, desperately longing for the safety of home.

Yet, even in the midst of the storm, a flicker of hope remained. Deep down, I held on to the belief that God was my refuge, my safe place amidst the chaos. Reflecting on that day, I'm reminded of the profound power of faith and hope. Even when life feels like a relentless storm, we can take refuge in Him, bring our tears and fears to Him, and find comfort in His presence.

Psalm 16:1 reassures us that God is our anchor and our refuge, no matter how turbulent the storm.

Reflection Questions:

1. How do you seek God as your refuge during times of uncertainty and chaos?
2. What moments of clarity have you experienced amid life's storms?
3. How can you maintain hope and trust in God, even when faced with rejection and disappointment?

Conclusion:

Even when the storm seems unrelenting and our hearts heavy, God remains our steadfast refuge. Embrace the comfort and safety He offers, knowing that even in the fiercest of trials, His presence is your anchor. Hold on to hope, and trust that He will guide you through the storm, offering peace and renewal along the way.

Day 3

Embracing New Beginnings

Revelation 21:5 really hits home for me: *"He who was seated on the throne said, 'I am making everything new.'"*

Let me paint a picture for you: My car was still in the shop, and my husband, always the supportive partner, offered to drive me to a podcast recording I had scheduled. I'll admit, I wasn't exactly in the mood. My week had been a whirlwind, and faking a cheerful demeanor felt like climbing a mountain. But as soon as I stepped into the studio, I was greeted by someone whose warmth was like a ray of sunshine piercing through my clouds. We had a pre-recording chat, and I found myself opening up about my struggles. She listened with such empathy, prayed with me, and handed me a small devotional—almost like she knew I needed it before I did. I tucked it away, feeling a flicker of hope.

During the recording, I shared how my faith had been my anchor through the stormy seas of life and the peace I've found in God's unshakeable presence. After we wrapped up, the sound engineer approached me with a heavy heart. He shared that he and his wife had just experienced a miscarriage and was eager to show her the episode, hoping it would bring some comfort. It was a profound moment, revealing how God had orchestrated our meeting to provide solace and encouragement in our shared pain.

When I got home, my daughter suggested a movie night, which was a welcome break. As I waited for her to get ready, I pulled out that devotional. The very first entry was titled "New Beginnings," and the verse from Revelation 21:5 was staring back at me. I couldn't believe it. I rushed to show my husband, and we stood in awe, realizing that even amidst the swirling uncertainty, God's presence was a constant reminder to shift our focus from what's broken to the new things He's creating in our lives.

Reflection Questions:

1. How have unexpected encounters—like the woman at the studio and the sound engineer—shifted your perspective on your current struggles?
2. When you come across messages of "New Beginnings," how do they resonate with your own experiences and challenges?
3. In what ways can you find comfort and reassurance in God's presence, even when life feels unpredictable and uncertain?

Conclusion:

Even when the path ahead seems unclear and our hearts are heavy, God is at work, making all things new. Embrace these moments of unexpected encouragement and let them remind you of the new beginnings He's crafting for you. Hold on to hope, and trust that through every challenge, His presence is guiding and renewing you.

Day 4

Trusting the Beauty of God's Timing

Ecclesiastes 3:11 reminds us: "*God makes everything beautiful in its own time. He's put a sense of eternity in our hearts, but we can't figure out what He's up to from start to finish.*"

The sun was just starting to rise when the weight of uncertainty hit me hard. I felt like I was carrying a ton of bricks, my body aching with the burden of it all. I knew I needed some fresh air and sunshine, so I forced myself out of bed, with Churro, our enthusiastic pup, eagerly tagging along. Normally, I'd slip on my earbuds and listen to a podcast or some tunes during my morning stroll. But today, I craved silence. My mind was a swirl of thoughts.

There were job opportunities popping up left and right, promising security and validation, but something didn't sit right. With less than a month left at my current job, I felt drained and the idea of trusting God's plan seemed overwhelming.

I had a podcast recording scheduled for the afternoon, even though I wasn't really in the mood for it. But seeing Heather's friendly face on the screen was a comfort. Our conversation about finding our true selves lifted my spirits. Yet, as evening approached, sadness swept over me like a tidal wave—clarity drowned in tears.

Then, a call from my mentor, Debbie, was like a beacon of light. It felt like God was sending these little moments to remind me He was there, watching over me. And then, as night fell, my daughter's boyfriend pointed out a rare display of the northern lights—a breathtaking reminder of God's power and control. Standing under that celestial masterpiece, I felt like I was wrapped in a heavenly hug, a tangible sign that even in the chaos, God was at work, crafting something beautiful. In that moment, I felt God whisper, "Do you trust me?"

Reflection Questions:

1. How did your interactions with Heather, Debbie, and witnessing the northern lights reinforce your belief in God's presence and guidance?
2. How did the quiet of your morning walk help you process your thoughts and feelings during a time of uncertainty?
3. What steps can you take to deepen your trust in God's timing and plan, especially when facing challenging transitions?

Conclusion:

Remember, even in the midst of confusion and uncertainty, God is at work, making everything beautiful in its own time. Trust that He is crafting something wonderful in your life, and let His quiet whispers guide you through the chaos. Embrace the beauty of His timing, and find comfort in the knowledge that He is always with you.

Day 5

Embracing the Unexpected

Isaiah 41:13 says, *"I am God, and I'll hold your hand tight, telling you not to worry because I've got your back."* It's like a warm hug from God, a reminder that He's always there to ease our fears and guide us through the tough spots.

Let me share a moment from my life. It was strawberry season, and my daughter was bubbling with excitement about the festival. I was feeling a bit all over the place, unsure if I wanted to commit to the plans. So, I told her I'd decide in the morning. When the sun came up, I chose to embrace the moment and go for it. Even though I was still working on staying present and not letting worries about the future take over, I decided to give it a shot. I quietly asked God to be with us as we headed out.

When we arrived at the festival, the parking lot was packed. Instead of letting it ruin our day, we decided to adapt. Sushi sounded like a great alternative, so we set out to explore without a set plan. We ended up at Home Goods, one of my favorite spots to wander. It wasn't what we originally planned, but we ended up having a fantastic time. Sometimes, letting go and going with the flow turns out to be exactly what we need.

Looking back, I realize it's okay when things don't go as planned. Embracing the unexpected can lead to delightful surprises and new memories. It's a reminder that the best moments often come from being present and open to what life throws our way.

Reflection Questions:

1. How does the verse from Isaiah 41:13 resonate with your own experiences of reassurance and support?

2. Can you recall a time when a change of plans led to an unexpectedly positive experience? What happened, and how did it make you feel?

3. What's one small step you can take today to focus more on living in the present and letting go of worries about the future?

Conclusion:

Today, let's remember that God's got our back. Sometimes, when plans go awry, it's an invitation to embrace the unexpected and find joy in the moment. Trust that even in the unplanned detours, there's a chance for beautiful surprises.

Day 6

Finding Joy in the Bittersweet

Hebrews 11:1 clarifies that, "*Now faith is the assurance of things hoped for, the conviction of things not seen.*"

The sun was blazing through my window as I woke up this Mother's Day, and I could feel its warmth on my face. Yet, it's always a bittersweet day for me. I celebrate the day, but my heart aches as I remember my daughter, who passed away in 2002. It's a day filled with a mix of joy and sorrow.

I got up, brewed my coffee, and took some time to journal before hopping in the shower to get ready for church. I was really hoping for some encouragement today, especially after the rough week I'd had.

Walking into church, I immediately felt a comforting sense of God's presence. The worship was moving, and I could feel my spirit lifting. Then the speaker began to talk about trust in Jesus—something I've been struggling with lately. I almost laughed out loud because it felt like God was speaking directly to me. The message was about living with courage through pain, how our faith is tested to build perseverance, and keeping our eyes on God's promises. It was exactly the boost I needed. I left church feeling uplifted and ready to face the day with renewed hope.

That evening, we celebrated Mother's Day with my family—my brother and his family, as well as my parents. After dinner, we followed our cherished tradition of "edification," where we take turns sharing heartfelt words about the person being honored. We do this for every birthday and special occasion. While I didn't always appreciate it growing up, I've come to see its importance. Life is precious and unpredictable, and I want those closest to me to know how much they are loved. After sharing these sweet words, tears were shed, and we enjoyed some cake and laughter. It turned out to be a beautiful day, a much-needed break from a tough week, finding joy even amidst the challenges.

Reflection Questions:

1. How do you find strength and encouragement during difficult periods?
2. What practices or experiences help you build and maintain trust in your faith journey?
3. Do you have any family traditions that are especially meaningful to you? How do they impact your life?

Conclusion:

Finding joy and encouragement during tough times can be challenging, but it's often through these moments that we discover the depth of our faith and the strength we didn't know we had. Embracing traditions that remind us of our loved ones and bring us together can offer comfort and perspective. As you navigate your own emotional landscapes, remember that your faith, combined with the love and support of those around you, can guide you through even the most challenging days. Embrace the moments of joy and let them uplift you, knowing that each day is a step forward in your journey of hope and healing.

Day 7

Embracing the Storm and Trusting the Journey

I woke up to the rumble of thunder, and the gloomy, stormy weather seemed to echo my own mood. Lately, it feels like every day brings a whirlwind of emotions, and the dreary weather didn't do much to lift my spirits. I had interviews and a full day of coaching meetings ahead, and getting out of bed felt like a monumental task. I'm working towards getting certified as a financial coach, and honestly, all I wanted was to stay cozy under the blankets. But I knew that pushing through would be worth it in the end.

One of the calls I was really excited about was with a company that specializes in corporate coaching. I had prepared thoroughly, and thankfully, the meeting went well. This organization aligns perfectly with my passions and goals. However, they're a startup and were upfront about not being able to meet my salary expectations. After the call, I found myself praying, "God, if this is where you want me, please make a way for me to work with them." Today, I'm embracing the challenge of praying boldly and trusting that God understands our financial needs. For the first time, I'm consciously trying to let go of my need to control everything and allowing God to take the lead.

Even though it's tough, this process of letting go and trusting is teaching me a lot about faith and patience. It's not just about finding a job but about aligning with what truly matters and waiting for the right doors to open.

Reflection Questions:

1. How do my current feelings shape my daily choices and actions? Do they push me towards or away from my goals?
2. What are the benefits of pushing through tough moments, even when I'm not feeling motivated or enthusiastic?
3. How can I balance pursuing my passions with addressing my practical financial needs?
4. What does it mean to let go of control and trust a higher power in making decisions about my career and future?
5. How can I remain open to new opportunities, even if they don't meet all of my expectations right away?

Conclusion:

Facing uncertainty and challenging moments can feel overwhelming, but they also offer a chance for growth and deeper trust. By pushing through the tough days and remaining open to new possibilities, you're not just navigating through your career or personal challenges—you're learning to align with a greater plan. Trusting that there's a path unfolding for you, even if it's not immediately clear, can bring peace and confidence. So, embrace the journey, hold on to your faith, and let each step forward be a testament to your resilience and hope.

Day 8

Trusting the Open Door

Matthew 7:8 says, *"For everyone who asks receives, and the one who seeks finds, and to the one who knocks, the door will be opened."*

Here I am, nearly a week into what I'm calling the "no plan B" phase, and it's starting to sink in. Wrapping up a job I've been in for 28 years feels surreal. The uncertainty of what comes next is genuinely unsettling. It's a bit like going back to 2002, a year that tested me in ways I'd never imagined. I lost my daughter that year and then got laid off just eight weeks later. I keep reminding myself that this time is different. I've grown and learned so much since then, and I'm now a seasoned professional.

I've got job offers and have been on more interviews in the past week than I ever thought possible. But now, I'm asking myself what I truly want. It would be easy to settle for a comfortable job, but I'm at a crossroads. I'm seeking guidance and trusting God to show me the way. With so many people offering advice, God tells me to focus solely on His voice and direction. It's about stepping out of my comfort zone and trusting His plan, even though I can't see it just yet.

Amid this uncertainty, I'm learning to lean on faith and trust that everything will unfold as it should.

Reflection Questions:

1. Have you ever had to fully trust in a plan or outcome you couldn't clearly see? How did that experience shape you?
2. What are some key lessons or strengths you've gained from past challenges?

3. How do you decide which advice to follow and which to set aside in times of uncertainty?

4. What practical steps can you take to better tune into your inner guidance or spiritual direction?

Conclusion:

Navigating through uncertainty can be daunting, but it's also a chance to deepen your faith and trust in a greater plan. As you explore your own path, remember that each step, even when unclear, is part of a journey toward growth and discovery. Trust that you're being guided and supported in ways you might not yet understand. By focusing on what feels right for you and listening to your inner guidance, you can move forward with confidence and hope.

Day 9

Art of Rebuilding

"For everything there is a season, and a time for every matter under heaven... a time to break down, and a time to build up." — Ecclesiastes 3:1,3

There are moments in life when it feels like the only option is to bulldoze everything and start over. Sometimes life falls apart in ways we never expected, and all that's left to do is tear down what was and rebuild something new. It's not easy, but it's necessary for growth.

Over the past four years, it seems like I've been living in a constant cycle of tearing down and rebuilding. When we decided to move to Tennessee, I knew it wouldn't be smooth sailing. I even wrestled with God about it—leaving everything familiar in California to move across the country? That wasn't part of *my* plan. But deep down, I knew staying wasn't an option either. Still, the transition was far from easy. Our oldest child was struggling, and our youngest was in their senior year of high school. Honestly, the timing felt completely wrong.

I tried to trust that God would restore our hearts amid the move, but what I didn't expect was how much we would have to rebuild our entire lives—our family dynamic, our friendships, and even our faith. The first few months were lonely and filled with doubt. Even though we made some amazing connections in Tennessee, I couldn't help but question why God moved us so far away from everything that felt like home. My identity and worth seemed tangled up in what I had left behind. That's when God started to work on my heart, whispering, *It's time to rebuild.*

Restoration is a beautiful concept—it feels safe, almost like a fresh coat of paint that makes things look new again. But rebuilding? That's different. Rebuilding requires demolition, tearing down the things that no longer serve us, so that something new can rise. It's not just fixing what's broken; it's starting from scratch. It's hard, messy, and it forces you to confront areas of your life that are tough to face.

Think of it like this: when you restore an old chair, you sand it, prime it, and repaint it so it looks good again. But if that chair is falling apart, restoration isn't enough—you have to rebuild it. You take it apart, piece by piece, and put it back together stronger than before. That's what God's been doing in me these past few years. Every part of my life—my marriage, my relationships, my faith—needed to be taken apart and rebuilt.

Even my marriage had to be rebuilt from the ground up. My husband and I revisited the early days of our relationship, delving into our pasts and identifying things we carried into our marriage that needed to be torn down. It was uncomfortable and at times exhausting. But now, in the middle of this rebuilding process, I can see that the hard work is worth it. We're stronger because of it.

Rebuilding may feel overwhelming, but it's also an opportunity to create something stronger and more beautiful than what was there before. I'm still in the process, but I'm learning to trust that God's blueprint for my life is far better than anything I could have planned. There is beauty in the mess, and I'm choosing to trust that the rebuilding is all part of His plan.

Reflection Questions:

1. Is there an area of your life where you've resisted change because it feels uncomfortable? How might God be inviting you to rebuild in that space?
2. What "walls" in your life need to come down so that God can build something new and better for you?
3. How can you lean on God during your season of rebuilding, trusting Him to guide you through the process?

Conclusion:

Embracing the season of rebuilding is not just about enduring the difficulty but also about welcoming the potential for renewal and growth. As you navigate through this challenging time, remember that each step in the rebuilding process is shaping you for a stronger, more resilient future. Trust that God's plan is unfolding in ways you may not yet see, and allow His guidance to lead you toward a renewed sense of purpose and hope. The journey might be tough, but the beauty that emerges from the rebuilding will be a testament to His grace and your perseverance.

Day 10

Trusting God's Timing

"For I know the plans I have for you," declares the Lord, "plans to prosper you and not to harm you, plans to give you hope and a future." — Jeremiah 29:11

Waiting for a breakthrough can feel like an endless battle, right? I know that deep exhaustion that makes you want to just crawl under the covers and hide from it all. Sometimes, it feels like the more you pray and wait, the heavier the burden becomes. The storm doesn't seem to let up, and the waiting feels unbearable. But even when it feels like you've got nothing left to give, we can't stay buried in that darkness. God calls us to rise, to trust Him, and keep going because He has a purpose waiting for us on the other side of the pain.

When you're in the thick of a tough season, it's easy to feel weak, scared, and maybe even forgotten. The weight of everything can be overwhelming, and sometimes you wonder if you'll ever see the light again. But here's what I want to gently remind you of today: this is just a season. And the thing about seasons? They don't last forever. While this one may feel long and never-ending, there's a promise on the other side—a promise of something better, something more beautiful than you can imagine right now.

Think about a tiny seed planted deep in the soil. It's buried in the dark, surrounded by the pressure of the earth, struggling to break through. It can't see the light yet, but still, it pushes upward. It keeps going, pressing through the dirt because it knows there's something greater waiting ahead. Eventually, it breaks through and grows into something strong, something that bears fruit. Just like that seed, you're pressing through your own dark soil—the pain, the frustration, the heartbreak. But you, too, will break through. And when you do, you'll look back and realize that every tear and every moment of struggle wasn't wasted. There was a purpose in it all.

So today, hold on to hope. Your breakthrough is coming. And when it does, you'll be stronger, more resilient, and more grateful than ever before.

Reflection Questions:

1. What areas of your life right now feel heavy, like you're buried under the weight of hardship?
2. How can you remind yourself that this tough time is just a season, and like all seasons, it will eventually change?
3. What does it look like for you to trust God with your pain, knowing that He's working everything for your good, even when it doesn't feel like it?
4. How might this current struggle be preparing you for the purpose and blessings waiting on the other side?
5. What's one small step you can take today to push through the "soil" and move closer to your breakthrough?

Conclusion:

Keep pressing on, knowing that God's plan for you is good, even when it's hard to see right now. Embrace the hardship of every obstacle as an exercise to test and strengthen both your faith and character. Your breakthrough is ahead!

Day 11

When "No" Means "Not Yet"

"For my thoughts are not your thoughts, neither are your ways my ways," *declares the Lord. "As the heavens are higher than the earth, so are my* *ways higher than your ways and my thoughts than your thoughts."* — Isaiah 55:8-9

Sometimes, when God says "no," it feels like He's slammed a door shut on something we deeply hoped for, doesn't it? We cling to the belief that a "yes" is just around the corner, or that the delay is only temporary. I remember back in 2021, someone gave me a prophetic word—a promise that filled my heart with so much hope and anticipation. I thought the fulfillment was just around the corner. Yet, here I am, three years later, still waiting. The promise hasn't come to pass, and in those quiet moments, doubt likes to creep in. Did I misunderstand? Did I do something wrong?

But even in those moments of doubt, I've realized something important: God's promises don't have an expiration date. His "no" doesn't mean "never." It's a hard truth to accept sometimes. The waiting, the wondering, the silence—it can be tough to hold onto faith when things aren't unfolding the way we hoped. But God, in His infinite wisdom, often takes us on a journey through challenging seasons—valleys of uncertainty and paths that feel rocky and uncomfortable—because He is preparing us for something we can't yet see.

In these times, how we respond matters. Do we throw up our hands in frustration and question His goodness? Or do we stand firm, trusting that God sees the bigger picture, even when we don't? Philippians 3:8

reminds us that everything else pales in comparison to knowing Christ. When we shift our focus from "when" and "why" to the beauty of trusting and knowing Him, even the longest seasons of waiting become more bearable. It doesn't mean the waiting is easy, but it does mean we can find peace in the process.

If you're in a season of waiting—if God's "no" has left you feeling uncertain—know this: His "no" might just be a "not yet." There's purpose in the waiting, even when it's hard to see. Stand firm. Be patient. Keep your eyes on Him, and trust that He is working behind the scenes. His timing is always perfect, and His plans for you are so much greater than you can imagine.

Reflection Questions:

1. Can you think of a time when God's "no" or "not yet" felt hard to accept? How did you react in that moment?
2. How do you typically handle seasons of waiting? What emotions or thoughts come up for you during those times?
3. How might you shift your focus away from unmet expectations and instead deepen your relationship with Christ during this season?
4. What do you think God might be trying to teach you or prepare you for in your current season of waiting?
5. How can you remind yourself that God's promises are trustworthy, even when they don't happen on your timeline?

Conclusion:

Remember, His "no" isn't the end of the story. It's often the beginning of something better. Keep trusting in His perfect timing.

Day 12

Finding Calm in Life's Storms

"But He said to them, 'Why are you fearful, O you of little faith?' Then He arose and rebuked the winds and the sea, and there was a great calm."*— Matthew 8:26 (NKJV)

Last night's storm was intense. The wind howled like someone was throwing golf balls against my window. As chaotic as it was, I've come to appreciate the way Southern storms roll in and blow out just as quickly. There's a strange comfort in knowing the storm will pass, even if it shakes the house for a bit.

This morning, lying in bed, I found myself thinking about how life's storms are a lot like that. When we're in the middle of a tough season, it feels like it'll never end. The rain pours, the winds whip, and there's no clear end in sight. I wish life's storms passed as quickly as real ones, but they often linger longer than we want.

So, how do we handle those drawn-out struggles? I'll be honest—I haven't always been the best at staying positive when life gets hard. I've had my share of tears, frustration, and confusion. But as I've walked through my healing journey, I've learned not to let the storm consume me. It doesn't mean I have it all figured out—I still have moments of anger and sadness—but I'm learning to anchor myself in gratitude, trust in God's plan, and rest in Him.

The story in Matthew 8:24-27 is such a powerful reminder of the peace Jesus brings. The disciples were panicking, convinced the storm was going to drown them, while Jesus was calmly asleep. When they woke Him, He simply rebuked the storm, and instantly, everything was calm.

That's the kind of peace He can bring into our lives—no matter how fierce the storm is, Jesus is in control. He can speak calm into our chaos, and we don't have to be afraid, even when everything feels out of control.

Reflection Questions:

1. How do you react when you're going through a storm in life? Take a moment to notice your emotions. Are you overwhelmed, anxious, or trying to stay calm? Understanding your initial reactions can help you navigate through the storm with more clarity.

2. Do you find it hard to trust Jesus during your toughest moments? Reflect on your faith journey. When things get rough, is it challenging to believe that Jesus is in control? What could help you lean into His peace and trust Him more?

3. If you're in a storm right now, does it remind you of past challenges? Consider whether your current struggles echo previous ones. Recognizing these patterns might offer insights into how you've handled things before and how you can move forward now.

Conclusion:

As you think through these questions, know that storms don't last forever. Just like in Matthew 8, Jesus is with you, ready to bring peace to your heart, even in the middle of the chaos.

Day 13

God's "No"—Not Rejection, But Protection

No is a word I've heard a lot in my life, especially in sales. It's just part of the job. Every sales training tells you to get used to hearing it, but that's always been hard for me. Rejection has always been my deepest wound, so you can imagine how challenging it is to work in sales, where rejection comes with the territory. They say that with every "no," you're one step closer to a "yes," but for someone like me, that "no" can sting every single time.

Sometimes, I think we approach God the same way we do clients. We keep asking, hoping that if we ask enough, He'll change His mind. But God isn't like a client we can negotiate with. Sometimes His "no" isn't just a delay—it's a final answer. And that can feel like the ultimate rejection, leaving us wondering why He closed the door and whether He's left us altogether.

But over the years, God has gently shown me that His "no" isn't about rejecting me at all—it's about protecting me. I'll be honest, it's still hard to accept that in the moment, especially when all I want is a "yes." But more often than not, God is saving me from something I can't see, something that would've hindered me rather than helped me.

Romans 8:28 reminds us, *"And we know that in all things God works for the good of those who love Him, who have been called according to His purpose."* When a door closes, it's not because God has rejected you. It's because He sees what's ahead and is working for your good— even when it doesn't feel like it.

God's "no" isn't rejection. It's His love, His care, His protection over you. And that's something we can trust, even when it's hard to understand.

Reflection Questions:

1. Where in your life have you felt God's "no"? How did it impact you at the time?
2. Can you look back and see a time when a closed door actually protected you from something harmful?
3. How can you shift your perspective today to see God's "no" as an act of love and protection rather than rejection?

Conclusion:

God's love for you never wavers, even in His "no." Trust His heart, even when the answer is hard to hear.

Day 14

Protection in the "No"

Scripture:

"The Lord is good, a refuge in times of trouble. He cares for those who trust in Him."— Nahum 1:7 (NIV)

We've all heard that phrase, "Rejection is God's protection," but when you're on the receiving end of that "no," it can be hard to see how it's protective at all. In the moment, it feels more like disappointment, frustration, or even confusion. But God's "no" often shields us from things we can't see. It's His loving way of steering us away from potential dangers or heartache that we might not even know exist.

Take relationships, for example. You might have prayed for a friendship or a romantic relationship to work out, only to feel heartbroken when it didn't. At the time, you couldn't understand why. But then, months or even years later, you realize that if that relationship had continued, it would have led you into a place of pain, insecurity, or distraction from your purpose. God was protecting your heart by saying "no" and clearing the way for something healthier.

Or think about a job opportunity that seemed like *the* perfect next step for your career. You were so ready for that "yes," but the door closed unexpectedly. You were left wondering why God would hold back something you were so excited about. Yet later, you find out that the company was unstable, or the work environment was toxic. That "no" protected you from entering a situation that could have drained you emotionally, spiritually, or even physically.

God sees what we can't. He knows the road ahead. So when He closes a door or says "no," it's not because He's holding out on you. It's because He's lovingly keeping you from something that would hurt you, something that might pull you off the path He's prepared for you.

We don't always get the benefit of seeing the full picture. Sometimes we never know what God was protecting us from. But that's where faith comes in. We trust that His "no" is a shield, not a punishment. His love is so deep that He'd rather see us temporarily disappointed than permanently wounded.

So, the next time you're faced with a "no," remember: it could very well be God's hand of protection over your life, sparing you from an unseen danger.

Reflection Questions:

1. Can you think of a time when God said "no" and, in hindsight, you realized He was protecting you from something harmful? How does that shape your perspective on His "no" in other areas of your life?
2. How do you handle disappointment when you feel like God has closed a door? What steps can you take to trust His protection more fully in those moments?
3. In what areas of your life are you currently waiting for an answer from God? How can you trust that even if He says "no," it's out of love and protection for you?

Conclusion:

God's "no" is His way of wrapping His arms around you, keeping you safe from what you don't even see. Trust His protection—it's always for your good.

Day 15

God's "No" is a Detour, Not a Dead End

"Many are the plans in a person's heart, but it is the Lord's purpose that prevails."— Proverbs 19:21 (NIV)

We've all been there. You pray for something, believing it's the best thing for you. Your heart is set on it. But then God says, "No." That "no" can feel like a rejection, like the end of the road. But what if it's not? What if God's "no" is simply a detour, rerouting you to something far better than you ever imagined?

Think about Jonah. God told him to go to Nineveh, but Jonah had other plans. He said "no" to God and ended up in the belly of a great fish. Talk about a detour! But that detour wasn't the end of Jonah's story. It redirected him back to the purpose God had for him. He eventually went to Nineveh and became part of something far greater than his initial plans.

Then there's Joseph. God allowed him to be sold into slavery, falsely accused, and thrown into prison. Each setback seemed like a "no" to his dreams. But every "no" was actually preparing him for something better. In the end, Joseph became second in command in Egypt, saving countless lives—including his own family.

God's "no" often feels painful in the moment, but it's not a dead end. It's a loving redirection. Maybe you're waiting on a promotion that hasn't come through. Or perhaps a relationship you've poured yourself into didn't turn out as you hoped. In those moments, it's easy to think that God's withholding something from you. But trust that His "no" is guiding you toward something even better.

God's plans for us are greater than we can comprehend. He sees the whole picture, while we're looking at one small piece. His "no" might be protecting us, preparing us, or positioning us for something greater. What feels like a closed door might be leading you to a wide-open field of opportunity that you never even imagined.

Take heart—God's "no" is never the end. It's a detour to something better.

Reflection Questions:

1. Can you think of a time in your life when God said "no" to something you really wanted? Looking back, how did that experience redirect you toward something better?
2. How do you usually respond when you feel like God is saying "no"? How might you change that response, knowing it's often a detour rather than a dead end?
3. In what areas of your life do you need to trust that God's "no" is preparing you for future blessings?

Conclusion:

Remember, God's plans for you are good—even when His answer is "no." Have faith in His wisdom and neverending love. Trust the detour.

Day 16

Learning Patience Through God's "No"

"But those who wait on the Lord shall renew their strength; they shall mount up with wings like eagles, they shall run and not be weary, they shall walk and not faint."— Isaiah 40:31 (NKJV)

Waiting on God is hard. When we want something so deeply, and the answer seems to be "no"—or maybe "not yet"—it can feel like we're stuck in a season of uncertainty. That waiting period can be frustrating, and if we're honest, we often feel like giving up. But here's the thing: God's "no" or "not yet" is often an invitation to grow in patience and trust. It's not always about denying us what we want but preparing us for something better in His perfect timing.

Isaiah 40:31 reminds us that those who wait on the Lord will renew their strength. It doesn't say those who rush ahead or try to take control will find peace—it says those who *wait*. It's in that waiting where we develop a deeper dependence on God. Patience is like a muscle; the more it's tested, the stronger it becomes.

Think about how many stories in the Bible are marked by waiting. Abraham waited for years for the promised son, Sarah. Joseph spent time in prison before stepping into his destiny. Even David, who was anointed as king, had to wait through years of hardship and trials before taking the throne. Each of these moments of waiting wasn't wasted. God was using that time to prepare their hearts, build their character, and strengthen their faith.

When God says "no" or "not yet," it's easy to feel like He's forgotten about us or that He's not listening. But often, He's actually teaching us patience and molding us for what's coming next. He sees the whole picture, and He knows the right time for everything. While we may be eager to see the end result, God is focused on the journey and the growth that happens along the way.

It's in the waiting that we learn to trust God's timing over our own. We may not always understand why we have to wait, but we can rest in the truth that God's delays aren't denials. They're part of His loving process of shaping us into who He's called us to be.

So, if you're in a season where God's "no" feels more like a "not yet," hold on. He's renewing your strength. He's preparing you. And when the time is right, you'll soar like eagles—stronger, wiser, and more faithful than before.

Reflection Questions:

1. What has been your experience with waiting on God's timing? How has it tested your patience, and how have you grown through it?
2. Can you think of a time when God's "not yet" led to a greater blessing than you expected? How did that experience deepen your faith?
3. How do you handle uncertainty when you don't know why God is saying "no" or "not yet"? What steps can you take to lean into His strength during these times of waiting?

Conclusion:

Remember, waiting on God isn't passive—it's a time of strengthening, growing, and preparing for what's ahead. Trust His timing, because it's always perfect.

Day 17

God's "No" is Rooted in Love

"For the Lord disciplines those he loves, as a father the son he delights in."
— Proverbs 3:12

Hearing "no" from God can sometimes feel like a gut punch, especially when our plans seem to crumble before our eyes. It's as if the very foundation of our hopes is being shaken. But what if we could reframe this "no" as a sign of divine care rather than rejection? What if we saw it as a loving intervention from a Father who knows what's best for us?

Just as a parent says "no" to protect a child or guide them away from danger, God's refusals are deeply rooted in His love for us. Proverbs 3:11-12 reminds us: "My son, do not despise the Lord's discipline, and do not resent his rebuke, because the Lord disciplines those he loves, as a father the son he delights in." Much like a parent's "no" can steer a child toward safety or a better path, God's "no" is motivated by His desire for our ultimate good and well-being.

I'm reminded of a time when I was fervently praying for something that felt like the answer to all my dreams. I was convinced it was meant to be, yet, despite my hopes, I faced repeated disappointments and closed doors. Each "no" felt like a personal blow, but in hindsight, I see those refusals as God's way of guiding me toward something even better— something I couldn't have anticipated at the time.

Understanding that God's "no" comes from a place of love can transform how we handle disappointment. Instead of feeling abandoned, we can find comfort in knowing that His plans for us are crafted with care and affection. As we discussed on Day 10, Jeremiah

29:11 assures us: "For I know the plans I have for you," declares the Lord, "plans to prosper you and not to harm you, plans to give you hope and a future." This reminder helps us trust that God's refusals are not denials but redirections toward something greater.

Reflection Questions:

1. Can you think of a time when God's "no" was particularly painful or disappointing? How might recognizing His love behind that "no" shift your view of the situation?
2. How do you usually react to God's refusals? What emotions or thoughts arise during those moments?
3. What are some practical ways to remind yourself of God's love and care when faced with a "no" or a closed door?
4. How can you cultivate trust in God's plan, especially when His answers diverge from your expectations?

Conclusion:

Accepting that God's "no" is rooted in love can profoundly change our approach to disappointment. Just as a loving parent guides their child with a "no," God's refusals come from a place of deep affection and concern for our well-being. As you encounter life's closed doors and unanswered prayers, remember that God's love is steadfast and His plans are always for your benefit. Trust in His perfect timing and find solace in the knowledge that every "no" is a step toward a larger, loving plan.

Day 18

Trusting in the Bigger Picture

*"For my thoughts are not your thoughts, neither are your ways my ways,"
declares the Lord. "As the heavens are higher than the earth, so are my
ways higher than your ways and my thoughts than your thoughts."*
— Isaiah 55:8-9

Have you ever been in a situation where God's "no" felt like a major
setback? It's tough when our plans and dreams seem to crumble, and it's
hard to understand why God would shut a door that seemed perfect for
us. Yet, these moments can be opportunities to trust in a much bigger
picture that we might not see right now.

Take Abraham, for instance. God promised him that he would be the
father of many nations (Genesis 17:4-5). Yet, Abraham waited for years,
facing the disappointment of not having a child until he was quite old.
Imagine the doubt he must have felt! But Abraham trusted in God's
promise, even when the timeline didn't make sense. His faith was
rewarded with the birth of Isaac, and ultimately, he became the father of
nations as promised.

Or consider David, anointed as king while still a young shepherd boy.
He faced numerous trials, including years of fleeing from King Saul,
who was jealous and sought to kill him. David had every reason to
question God's plan. Yet, he trusted that God had a bigger plan in mind
for him, and eventually, he became one of Israel's greatest kings.

These stories remind us that when God says "no," it's not the end of the
road but rather a redirection toward something greater. God's ways are
higher than ours, and His vision is far broader than our own. Just like

Abraham and David, we're called to trust in the bigger picture that God is painting, even if we can't yet see it.

Reflection Questions:

1. Can you think of a time when God's "no" felt like a roadblock in your life? How did you respond, and what did you learn from the experience?
2. How do the stories of Abraham and David inspire you to trust God's bigger plan for your life?
3. When faced with uncertainty or disappointment, what practical steps can you take to remind yourself of God's greater vision and timing?
4. How might your perspective change if you viewed God's "no" as a redirection rather than a rejection?

Conclusion:

Trusting in the bigger picture that God has for our lives can be challenging, especially when His "no" feels like a setback. Yet, stories like those of Abraham and David remind us that God's plans are always filled with purpose and promise. As you navigate through life's disappointments and redirections, remember that God sees the entire canvas, even when we can only see a small part of it. Trust in His higher ways, and have faith that His plan is always leading you toward something greater.

Day 19

Finding Peace in God's "No"

"Do not be anxious about anything, but in every situation, by prayer and petition, with thanksgiving, present your requests to God. And the peace of God, which transcends all understanding, will guard your hearts and your minds in Christ Jesus." — Philippians 4:6-7

It's never easy when God says "no," is it? Whether it's a job you didn't get, a relationship that didn't work out, or a dream that seems out of reach, facing a "no" can stir up a whirlwind of emotions. Yet, finding peace in those moments can be transformative, and it starts with surrendering our will to His.

Let me share a story that might resonate with you. A few years ago, I was set on starting a new business venture. I had everything planned out: the strategies, the marketing, the budget—everything felt right. But just as I was about to launch, unforeseen obstacles popped up. My initial reaction was frustration and disappointment. I felt like all my hard work was for nothing.

In the midst of this, I decided to take a step back and seek God's guidance. I began spending time in prayer, reflecting on Philippians 4:6-7, and asking for His peace to replace my anxiety. I also started meditating on Scripture, focusing on verses that reminded me of God's faithfulness and love. Slowly but surely, I began to find a sense of calm. I realized that God's "no" wasn't a rejection but a redirection. He was guiding me to a different path, one that would better align with His plans for me.

Here's how you can find peace when faced with God's "no":

1. Prayer: Bring your feelings and frustrations to God. Be honest about your disappointment but also open to His guidance. Prayer is a way to connect with God and seek His comfort.
2. Reflection: Take time to reflect on your situation. Ask yourself what you can learn from this experience and how it might be leading you toward something better.
3. Meditation on Scripture: Find verses that resonate with your current struggle. Meditate on them to shift your focus from your immediate disappointment to God's promises and peace.
4. Gratitude: Even in disappointment, find things to be thankful for. Gratitude can shift your perspective and help you see the blessings in your life, even amidst the "no."

Reflection Questions:

1. Can you recall a time when you faced God's "no" and struggled to find peace? How did you eventually find calm amidst the disappointment?
2. How can incorporating prayer and reflection into your response to God's "no" change your experience of that "no"?
3. What Scriptures bring you comfort during times of disappointment? How can you use them to help you find peace?
4. How might practicing gratitude help you find peace and acceptance in situations where God says "no"?

Conclusion:

Finding peace in God's "no" often requires us to surrender our will and embrace His greater plan. By turning to prayer, reflection, Scripture, and gratitude, we can navigate the disappointment with a sense of calm and trust in His perfect timing. Remember, God's "no" is not the end of the road but a step toward a path that He has perfectly designed for you. Embrace His peace, and trust that He is guiding you toward something better.

Day 20

When God's "No" Leads to Growth

"Not only so, but we also glory in our sufferings, because we know that suffering produces perseverance; perseverance, character; and character, hope." — Romans 5:3-4

Have you ever faced a situation where God's "no" seemed like a dead end, only to realize later it was the beginning of something new? I certainly have, and it's often through these moments of denial that we experience some of our most significant personal growth.

Let me share a story that might sound familiar. A few years ago, I was passed over for a promotion I had worked so hard for. I had put in extra hours, taken on challenging projects, and even sought feedback to improve. When the announcement came, and I wasn't chosen, I felt like all my efforts had been in vain. It was a crushing blow, and I struggled to understand why God would allow this to happen.

I remember sitting at my kitchen table, feeling a mix of frustration and confusion. It seemed unfair, and I questioned what I had done wrong. But as I sat there, I decided to do something different this time: I turned to Scripture and started reflecting on what God might be teaching me through this disappointment.

Romans 5:3-4 reminded me that suffering and setbacks often lead to growth. My "no" wasn't a punishment but a chance for me to build perseverance and character. As I looked back, I realized that the experience was pushing me to grow in ways I hadn't anticipated. I developed new skills, learned to handle setbacks more gracefully, and ultimately strengthened my faith. What seemed like a roadblock was a detour to a better path.

Here's how you can embrace God's "no" as an invitation to growth:

1. Reflect on the Experience: Take time to consider what the situation is teaching you. Are there areas where you can grow spiritually, emotionally, or mentally? Ask yourself how this experience might be preparing you for future opportunities.
2. Seek God's Guidance: Pray for understanding and wisdom. Ask God to reveal what He wants you to learn from the situation and how you can use it for personal development.
3. Embrace the Challenge: See obstacles as opportunities to strengthen your character and faith. Challenges can be the fertile ground where growth occurs, so approach them with an open heart.
4. Document Your Journey: Keep a journal of your thoughts, feelings, and lessons learned. Over time, you'll see how your experiences have shaped you and how God has been working in your life.

Reflection Questions:

1. Can you think of a time when God's "no" led to personal growth? How did that experience shape you?
2. How do you usually respond to obstacles or refusals? What emotions or thoughts arise during these times?
3. What are some ways you can seek God's guidance and wisdom when facing a "no"?
4. How can you shift your perspective to view setbacks as opportunities for growth rather than just disappointments?

Conclusion:

God's "no" can often feel like a setback, but it's important to remember that it's also an invitation for growth. By reflecting on our experiences, seeking God's guidance, embracing challenges, and documenting our journey, we can transform these moments of denial into opportunities for spiritual, emotional, and mental development. Trust that God's ways are higher than ours, and see His "no" as a step toward becoming the person He is calling you to be. Embrace the growth that comes from these experiences, and find peace in knowing that He is working all things for your good.

Day 21

God's "No" and the Power of Faith

"But without faith, it is impossible to please Him, for he who comes to God must believe that He is and that He is a rewarder of those who diligently seek Him." — Hebrews 11:6

Facing a "no" from God can feel like a heavy blow, especially when we've invested so much in our hopes and dreams. It's like working tirelessly on a project only to see it fall apart just before completion. Yet, it's often through these moments of divine denial that our faith has the opportunity to grow stronger and more resilient.

Let me share a story from my own experience that might resonate with you. When my husband and I were early in our marriage, we were determined to buy our dream home. We had saved diligently, researched extensively, and prayed earnestly, believing this house was where we were meant to start our next chapter.

Just as we were ready to make an offer, we got the crushing news: our savings weren't enough to secure the purchase. I remember feeling defeated and confused. We had put so much hope into this house, and now it seemed like everything was falling apart. The seller, who had come to know and like us, gave us a brass door knocker with our names on it and told us to hold onto it, assuring us that one day God would bless us with a home of our own.

Years later, as we looked back, we realized that God had something even better in store for us. We ended up buying a newer, more beautiful home, and we were able to put that door knocker on our new front door.

Reflecting on this, I'm reminded of Job's story from the Bible. Job faced immense suffering and loss but maintained his faith in God's greater plan. His story teaches us that even when we face profound disappointment, trusting in God's goodness and sovereignty can lead to eventual restoration and blessings.

Here's how you can find strength and faith when God says "no":

1. Reflect on Biblical Stories: Look at figures like Job, Joseph, and Abraham who faced challenges but grew in their faith through them. Their stories can offer inspiration and insight.
2. Embrace the Journey: Trust that God's timing and plans are perfect, even when it seems like a door is closing. This can be an opportunity for growth and redirection in your life.
3. Pray for Guidance and Peace: Ask God to help you find peace and clarity during times of disappointment. Prayer can help you stay focused on His promises and open your heart to His plans.
4. Stay Open to New Opportunities: Sometimes a closed door is God's way of guiding you toward something even better. Be open to new paths and trust that He is leading you in the right direction.

Reflection Questions:

1. Can you recall a time when a closed door or God's "no" in your life led to a better outcome or new opportunity?
2. How do you handle moments of disappointment or frustration when your plans don't go as expected?
3. What biblical story or figure resonates with you during times of rejection or delay? How does their experience inspire you in your journey?

4. How can you remind yourself of God's greater plan and purpose when you face closed doors or unanswered prayers?

Conclusion:

Understanding that God's "no" can lead to growth and new opportunities can transform how we handle disappointment. Just as Job's story demonstrates that suffering and setbacks can be part of a larger plan, our experiences with closed doors can lead to unexpected blessings and stronger faith. By reflecting on these stories, embracing the journey, praying for guidance, and staying open to new possibilities, we can navigate life's challenges with grace and trust. Remember, God's timing is perfect, and His plans are always for our ultimate good.

Day 22

Surrendering to God's Will

"Not my will, but Yours be done." — Luke 22:42

Let me share a story that might resonate with you, especially if you've ever faced unexpected delays or detours. A few years ago, my family and I were eagerly anticipating a trip to Costa Rica. We'd meticulously planned every detail and were excited to escape to a tropical paradise. The journey began smoothly: a pleasant breakfast at the AMEX lounge in San Francisco, followed by a flight to Houston, and then on to our final destination.

But, as with many travel plans, things didn't go as expected. Our flight from Houston to Costa Rica was delayed, then cancelled. With limited options and no immediate solution, it looked like we might be stuck in Houston overnight. Our luggage went missing, adding to the chaos. The next morning, we were bumped from the morning flight and finally managed to secure seats on an evening flight.

When we arrived in Costa Rica, our luggage was still missing. We had to travel to the resort without it, which was less than ideal. My daughter's medication was in that lost luggage, and she ended up getting very sick. It was a stressful situation that tested our patience and ability to adapt.

As we faced these challenges, I was reminded of the importance of patience. Much like a traveler waiting for a delayed flight, we often find ourselves in situations where we can't control the outcome. I had to let go of my frustration and surrender to the circumstances. We decided to visit the resort's gift shop, where we bought some necessary items and made the best of our time by enjoying the pool. Even though it wasn't the vacation we had envisioned, we chose to focus on the positives and embrace the moment.

This experience brings to mind how travelers often have to wait for delayed flights or deal with unexpected changes. Just as we must wait patiently for our flights or adapt to new travel plans, God calls us to trust in His timing and plan, even when things don't go as we hoped.

Here's how you can practice surrender and patience in the face of life's unexpected detours:

1. Embrace the Unexpected: Just as delays in travel can lead to unexpected discoveries or moments of relaxation, try to see life's detours as opportunities for growth and new experiences.
2. Seek Peace Through Prayer: When faced with delays or disappointments, turn to prayer for guidance and peace. Asking God for strength and perspective can help you navigate through challenging situations.
3. Reflect on Scripture: Verses like Luke 22:42 can remind you of the importance of surrendering to God's will. Let these scriptures guide your thoughts and provide comfort during difficult times.
4. Adapt and Enjoy: Make the best of your current situation, even if it wasn't what you planned. Like we did with our impromptu shopping and pool time, find joy in the present moment.

Reflection Questions:

1. Have you ever experienced a situation where things didn't go as planned? How did you respond, and what did you learn from it?

2. How do you handle moments of waiting or unexpected changes in your life? What helps you maintain patience and trust?
3. How can you apply the example of Jesus' surrender to your own experiences with life's detours?
4. What practical steps can you take to find peace and embrace the present moment, even when things don't go as planned?

Conclusion:

Surrendering to God's will can be challenging, especially when our plans are interrupted or we face unexpected delays. By embracing the moment, seeking peace through prayer, reflecting on Scripture, and adapting to new circumstances, we learn to trust in God's perfect timing and greater plan. Even when life's journey takes unexpected turns, remember that God's love and guidance are unwavering. Trust in His plan, and find comfort in knowing that every detour is part of a larger, loving design.

Day 23

Practical Ways to Handle God's "No"

"For my thoughts are not your thoughts, neither are your ways my ways," *declares the Lord. "As the heavens are higher than the earth, so are my* *ways higher than your ways and my thoughts than your thoughts."***
— Isaiah 55:8-9 (NIV)

Hey there, friend. I want to share a story that's deeply personal and might resonate with you if you've faced a tough "no" from God. A few years ago, my mom, daughter, and I embarked on a journey of fasting and praying for a situation in my daughter's life. We were hopeful and determined, believing that God would bring restoration and breakthrough.

Our dear friend joined us in prayer, and together we sought God's intervention. Yet, every time it seemed like we were making progress, the situation would take a turn for the worse. After months of dedicated prayer and fasting, my friend came to me and said, "Rhonda, I think God has heard us. Maybe it's time to stop fasting and celebrate with some cake."

Not long after, my mom received a clear message from God—restoration wasn't going to happen; His answer was a firm "no." Initially, I couldn't accept it. I was convinced that God was going to restore the situation, but the answer was unequivocally "no." It wasn't what I wanted to hear, but it was clear.

Four years later, I can see that God's "no" was actually for the best. While I may never fully understand why things happened the way they did, I trust that God's wisdom far surpasses mine. His plan, though not what I expected, was ultimately better than what I had hoped for.

Reflecting on God's No

Facing a "no" from God can be heart-wrenching, especially when you've prayed earnestly and believed for a different outcome. But often, His "no" redirects us toward something greater or protects us from something we might not yet understand.

Here are some practical ways to cope when you're dealing with God's "no":

1. Pray Honestly: Share your feelings openly with God. Express your disappointment, confusion, and even frustration. Being honest in your prayers can help you process your emotions and find comfort.

2. Seek Support: Talk to trusted friends or mentors who can offer perspective and encouragement. Sometimes, a different viewpoint can help you see God's plan more clearly.

3. Journal Your Experience: Writing down your thoughts and feelings can be a powerful way to work through your emotions. It can also help you reflect on how you've grown and what you've learned through the experience.

4. Serve Others: Focusing on helping others can provide a fresh perspective and bring fulfillment. Volunteering or offering support can shift your focus from your own disappointment to making a positive impact in someone else's life.

5. Embrace the Journey: Accepting that God's "no" might be guiding you toward a different path can be freeing. Trust that His plan is unfolding, even if it's not what you envisioned.

Reflection Questions

1. Have you ever experienced a "no" from God that felt particularly challenging? How did you handle it?
2. How can you incorporate these practical steps into your own journey of dealing with disappointment?
3. What are some ways you can shift your focus from your unmet desires to serving and supporting others?

Conclusion:

Dealing with God's "no" can be incredibly tough, especially when it's not the answer you were hoping for. Yet, it's often in these moments that we find new understanding and growth. By praying openly, seeking support, journaling, serving others, and embracing the journey, you can find peace even when things don't turn out as you had planned. Remember, God's "no" is not the end but a redirection toward something greater. Trust in His wisdom and know that He is with you every step of the way.

Day 24

Refined by God's "No"

In 2021, we found ourselves in a tough season, walking through the park, praying, and seeking God. I remember vividly listening to Refiner by Maverick City Music, a song that had become a source of comfort during that time. The lyrics discuss being refined, laying everything before God, and surrendering ourselves as a living sacrifice. It's a beautiful sentiment, but let's be honest—it's not easy to do. The idea of saying, "God, refine me, no matter what that looks like," requires a level of surrender that most of us aren't naturally comfortable with.

During that season, God said "no" to so many things we deeply wanted and thought were aligned with His plan for us. It was frustrating and confusing. We couldn't understand why the things we thought were good and even God-honoring were being shut down.

Looking back, I see now that His "no" wasn't rejection. It was refinement. We were being shaped, our faith deepened, and our dependence on Him grew. That season of "no" wasn't about punishment or withholding; it was about teaching us to trust God even when things didn't make sense. We were being refined in ways we couldn't see at the time—through deep soul-searching, through wrestling with our faith, and through finding peace in God's plan over our own.

In hindsight, I realized that the refining wasn't just about the things we didn't get but about who we were becoming through the process. It was in the struggle, the unanswered prayers, and the quiet "no" that God did His most transformative work in us.

1. Daily Surrender in Prayer: Start your day by asking God to refine you. Tell Him you trust His "yes," "no," and "wait" with the same faith.
2. Journaling Your Journey: Write down the areas where you've experienced God's "no" and reflect on how He's used that to refine you.
3. Celebrate Growth: Instead of focusing solely on what you didn't receive, celebrate the growth and transformation God is working in you through His refining process.

Reflection Questions:

1. Can you think of a time when God's "no" felt more like rejection than refinement? How do you view that season now?
2. How might God be refining you in your current season of life? Are there areas where He's calling you to trust Him more deeply?
3. How can you embrace God's refining process, even when it doesn't align with your expectations or desires?

Conclusion:

God's "no" is often hard to hear, but it's in those moments that He is refining us for something greater. When we choose to surrender and trust Him, we open ourselves up to the growth, strength, and deeper faith He is cultivating within us. It's okay to wrestle with His answers and feel the weight of disappointment, but don't let it stop there. Recognize that even in the "no," God is working for your good, refining your heart, and drawing you closer to Him.

Day 25

Navigating Lifequakes with Faith

"The Lord is my rock, my fortress and my deliverer; my God is my rock, in whom I take refuge, my shield and the horn of my salvation, my stronghold." – Psalm 18:2

I remember growing up in California, where earthquakes were just a part of life. I'd be in the middle of doing something—eating breakfast, reading a book—and suddenly the ground would start to tremble. At first, it was always small, just a little shift. But sometimes, the shaking would grow stronger, and I would freeze, my mind racing with questions. How bad is this going to get? Will the house stand? What if the "big one" finally hits?

Life has its own "quakes" too. They show up unannounced, rattling our sense of security, and we wonder if we'll be able to stand or if everything around us will come crashing down. These "lifequakes"—whether it's the loss of a job, a sudden health diagnosis, or a relationship falling apart—leave us shaken, unsure of what's next.

I've had my share of lifequakes. One of the most profound was losing my daughter years ago, a tremor that felt like it cracked the very foundation of my world. No amount of preparation could've kept me from feeling the aftershocks of that grief. But through the pain, I clung to the One who never wavered—God, my unshakable rock.

Just like in those California quakes, there are moments in life when you simply have to brace yourself, knowing that you can't control the shaking. But we can control where we anchor ourselves. When we place our trust in God, we realize that no matter how violent the quake, He will hold us steady. He doesn't promise to prevent the shaking, but He promises to be our refuge through it.

I've come to learn that these lifequakes, as disruptive and terrifying as they are, have a way of exposing what we're truly relying on. Is our foundation built on something temporary—like our careers, relationships, or achievements—or is it built on the eternal strength of God?

Reflection Questions:

1. What are some lifequakes you've experienced recently or in the past that shook your foundation?
2. When life starts to shake, where do you instinctively turn for security and comfort?
3. How can you begin to place your trust more firmly in God, even in the midst of uncertainty and fear?

Conclusion:

Lifequakes will happen. They are an inevitable part of our journey. But just as we prepare for physical earthquakes with safety plans and supplies, we can prepare for spiritual lifequakes by rooting ourselves in God's Word, seeking His presence daily, and remembering that He is our steadfast rock. So when the ground starts to tremble beneath your feet, don't panic. Anchor yourself in the One who cannot be moved, and trust that He will carry you through the shaking.

God is with you in every tremor, every aftershock. And though life may quake, His love never will.

Day 26

When God's "No" is About Rebuilding, Not Just Restoring

"And the God of all grace, who called you to his eternal glory in Christ, after you have suffered a little while, will himself restore you and make you strong, firm, and steadfast." – 1 Peter 5:10

We often approach life's challenges with a hope for restoration, wanting things to go back to the way they were. I remember when my daughter, mother, and I were fervently praying and fasting for a breakthrough. We were holding onto hope that God would restore what had been broken. But instead of restoration, we were given a "no."

At first, this felt like the ultimate disappointment—an unanswered prayer, a door slammed shut. We'd hoped God would restore the situation and bring things back to the way they were before. But over time, I realized something profound: God wasn't interested in merely restoring the old. He wanted to rebuild something entirely new in me.

There's a difference between restoring and rebuilding. Restoration is about going back to what once was—returning to familiar routines, habits, or relationships. It can be comforting to hope for things to return to a former state. But rebuilding is different. Rebuilding means creating something new after something has been dismantled. It's not about going back—it's about moving forward.

God's "no" wasn't about keeping me in a place of loss. It was about tearing down the old, flawed structures I was clinging to and rebuilding me into someone stronger, more resilient, and more anchored in Him. While restoration would've been comforting, rebuilding created a deeper transformation in my heart. It required me to let go of my plans and trust that God was creating something better.

Sometimes, we face moments when we want God to restore a relationship, a job, or a dream. But what if God's "no" is about rebuilding you into someone who can handle the new things He has planned? God isn't just in the business of returning us to the way things were. He's in the business of growth, renewal, and transformation.

Reflection Questions:

1. Is there an area of your life where you've been praying for restoration, but God seems to be saying "no"?
2. How does the idea of rebuilding—creating something new—change your perspective on a recent setback?
3. What old mindsets, habits, or expectations might God be asking you to let go of so He can rebuild something stronger in you?

Conclusion:

When God says "no," it can feel like a painful rejection of what we desperately want. But sometimes, His "no" is the beginning of a rebuilding process. It's an invitation to let go of the past and embrace something new, something stronger, something only He can create. Restoration might seem like the easier option—it offers comfort and familiarity. But rebuilding brings growth, transformation, and a deeper reliance on God.

The next time you face a "no," pause and ask God if He's leading you into a season of rebuilding. Trust that even though the process may be messy and uncomfortable, the result will be something far greater than you could've imagined.

God isn't just restoring what was; He's rebuilding who you are.

Day 27

Wrestling with the "No"

"Then the man said, 'Your name will no longer be Jacob, but Israel, because you have struggled with God and with humans and have overcome.'" – Genesis 32:28 (NIV)

I think we've all been there, pouring our hearts out to God, pleading for a different outcome, only to be met with silence or even a clear "no." It's such a hard place to sit, isn't it? The disappointment, frustration, and confusion can be overwhelming. But what if the "no" isn't just a final answer but an invitation to wrestle?

Jacob's story in Genesis 32 has always struck a chord with me. Here's a man who had spent his life fighting, fighting for his birthright, fighting to make a name for himself, and ultimately fighting with God. When Jacob wrestled with God, it wasn't a quick match. It lasted all night, long enough for him to walk away with a limp that would stay with him for the rest of his life. But through that wrestling, Jacob's name was changed to Israel, meaning "he struggles with God." It wasn't about defeating God but about being transformed through the struggle.

Isn't that what happens when we wrestle with God's "no"? We want what we want, and when God's response doesn't line up with our plans, we feel that tension. But maybe the wrestling is where the transformation happens. Maybe it's in the back-and-forth, the questions, the tears, and even the frustration, where God is shaping us into something new. Like Jacob, we may walk away with a limp, a reminder of the struggle, but also with a new understanding of who we are and who God is.

I've been in seasons of wrestling with God's "no." It's not easy, and I don't always get the answers I want. But what I've found is that God meets me in that place, not with condemnation but with compassion. He's not afraid of our questions or our struggles. In fact, He invites us to bring them to Him, to wrestle it out.

Reflection Questions:

1. 1.When have you experienced a "no" from God that led to a season of wrestling?
2. How did that wrestling shape or change your relationship with Him?
3. 3.What part of Jacob's story can you relate to most right now?

Conclusion:

Wrestling with God's "no" isn't about winning or losing; it's about being willing to engage with Him, to bring our full selves into the struggle. Like Jacob, we might not walk away unscathed, but we will walk away changed. And maybe, just maybe, that's the whole point. God's "no" could be the very thing that transforms us into who He's calling us to be. So, if you're in that place of wrestling today, remember, you're not alone—and the struggle itself might be the blessing in disguise.

Day 28

Hope Deferred: Finding Light in Waiting Seasons

"Hope deferred makes the heart sick, but a desire fulfilled is a tree of life."
– Proverbs 13:12

Have you ever experienced a season where you felt like all your hopes and prayers were met with silence? When we're holding onto something so deeply and it doesn't come to pass, it can feel like God is saying "no." And that "no" stings. But what if, in these moments of deferred hope, God is actually working something deeper in us—allowing us to hold onto hope, even when the outcome looks different than we expected?

In my last devotional, I shared about the death of our daughter, Tiana. It was one of the hardest moments of my life, especially when God revealed to my mom that the baby wasn't healthy and He was going to take her home to heaven. That wasn't something I wanted to hear. In the midst of my grief, though, I found a surprising source of hope. After Tiana passed, I felt this incredible sense of certainty that God would bless me with another baby one day.

I remember sitting with the doctor as she carefully asked me if I understood what had happened. She was worried I was in shock, but deep down, I had this unshakable hope. God had given me peace that I wasn't done being a mom. Month after month, though, as I wasn't getting pregnant, that hope was tested. It was hard, especially when my heart longed for another child. But even in the disappointment, I knew that God had planted that hope within me, and I held onto it.

Proverbs 13:12 speaks so clearly to this feeling: "Hope deferred makes the heart sick." When our expectations aren't met, it hurts. It can feel like a heavy weight in our chest, a longing that goes unanswered. But the verse doesn't end there—it also says that when a desire is fulfilled, it is a tree of life. This is the reminder that while waiting feels painful, God's timing brings life and beauty in ways we can't always see in the moment.

Sometimes, God's answer isn't "no," but "not yet." And in those waiting seasons, He invites us to hold onto hope, not because it's easy, but because He is faithful. Deferred hope doesn't mean we're abandoned or forgotten. It means God is still working.

Reflection Questions:

1. Is there an area of your life where you've been holding onto hope, but feel discouraged in the waiting?
2. How can you remind yourself of God's faithfulness when your hope feels deferred?
3. Have you ever experienced God fulfilling a desire in an unexpected way, bringing about a deeper understanding of His timing?

It's in those moments of delay that God grows something inside us, patience, trust, and a deeper reliance on Him. Waiting isn't wasted. It shapes us, transforms us, and draws us closer to God's heart. So if you're in a season where hope feels deferred, hold on. God is still moving, even if it's not in the way you expected. His plans are always for our good, and the fulfillment, when it comes, will be a tree of life.

Conclusion:

Hope deferred may make our hearts ache, but it also points us to a greater promise: that God is always at work, even when we can't see it. Keep trusting, keep hoping, and know that God's faithfulness never fails.

The hope you held onto for another child after losing Tiana was a seed planted by God. Even though the waiting was painful, that hope was what kept you standing in faith. Where is God asking you to trust Him with deferred hope in your life today?

Day 29

When God's "No" Feels Like Abandonment

"I have been a Christian a long time, and I know that often when God says no, we can feel like He has abandoned us. I want you to know that God is for us. When the 'no' happens, He often has a greater plan that we might not see this side of heaven."

This sentiment is one I've wrestled with time and time again. When God says no, it feels personal, like He's withholding something good. And, honestly, it can be confusing. I've spent countless hours arguing with God over His "no's." Why can't things just work out the way I hope? Why does it seem like every door I knock on remains closed? Sometimes, I'm blessed to see the beautiful redemption story that comes from those "no's." But there are other times, countless moments, where I'll never understand why God said no, and I've had to make peace with that.

Here's the thing I've learned: if you feel angry or disappointed in God because of His "no," it's okay. Your feelings are valid. It's natural to feel frustrated when life doesn't go the way we expect. One of the clearest memories I have is my dad, during one of my many temper tantrums with God, gently reminding me, "He is big enough to handle your anger and frustrations." God isn't scared off by our emotions. He welcomes them. He wants us to bring our broken hearts, questions, and even our anger to Him.

Psalm 34:18 reminds us that "The Lord is close to the brokenhearted and saves those who are crushed in spirit." When you're in the middle of grappling with God's "no," that is exactly when He draws close. He doesn't pull away from us in our moments of pain or disappointment. He holds us tighter.

Reflection Questions:

1. Is there a "no" from God that still makes you feel frustrated or disappointed? How can you bring those emotions to Him today?

2. Have you ever experienced a time where God's "no" led to something better than what you originally wanted? How did that shape your perspective of His plans?

3. In what ways can you lean on God during moments of confusion or disappointment, even when you don't understand His reasoning?

Conclusion:

It's okay if you don't have all the answers right now. There are some "no's" we may never understand this side of heaven, and that's hard to accept. But God never wastes our pain. He sees the bigger picture, and while that doesn't always make it easier, it reminds us that we're not alone in this journey. His plans are always for our good, even when it doesn't feel like it in the moment.

Don't be afraid to bring your anger, sadness, or confusion to God. He is big enough to handle it, and He loves you deeply, even when His answer is "no." You are seen, you are heard, and God is working—even in the unanswered questions. Keep trusting Him, even when it's hard, knowing that one day, we'll see the fullness of His plan, whether here on earth or in eternity.

Day 30

No Weapon Formed Against You Shall Prosper

Have you ever found yourself in a season that feels like a desert? A time when nothing seems to be moving, and you're left waiting, feeling stuck with no end in sight? Those seasons are hard—dry, lonely, and filled with questions. It's often in these desert seasons that we face a lot of "no's." We pray, we ask, we plead, but sometimes God's answer is still, "No." And that can feel so defeating.But even when the answer is no, or when we feel surrounded by challenges, God reminds us of His promise in Isaiah 54:17:

"No weapon formed against you shall prosper."

That verse doesn't promise a life without hardship or battles, but it does promise that those hardships won't succeed in breaking us. Even in the dry, desert seasons, no weapon formed against us can stand. God is with us, even when it feels like nothing is happening, and we can still bring praise in the middle of the waiting.What does it look like to bring praise when you're in a desert season? It means choosing to trust Him, even when you don't understand. It's lifting your voice, even when your heart feels weary. It's believing that He's walking right alongside you, even when you can't see the way forward.

Reflection Questions:

1. Have you recently faced a season that feels like a desert? How did it challenge your faith?
2. In what ways have you seen God show up in past desert seasons, even if the outcome wasn't what you expected?

3. How can you shift your focus to praise God in the middle of your current struggles?

Conclusion:

Often, a "no" from God feels like we've been left in the desert, but the truth is He never leaves us there alone. He is always with us, working in ways we can't see, protecting us from weapons that won't succeed. Even in the waiting, in the unknown, let's choose to bring praise. His plan is always good, and He's right there with us, guiding us through every desert season.

So, today, let's trust Him, lift up praise, and rest in the promise that no weapon formed against us shall prosper.

Day 31

Surprise! Sometimes God says Yes.

"This is the confidence we have in approaching God: that if we ask anything according to his will, he hears us. And if we know that he hears us—whatever we ask—we know that we have what we asked of him."
—1 John 5:14-15

We often wrestle with the question of when and why God says no or wait. But what about the moments when He says yes? Sometimes, His yes comes swiftly—healing happens, doors open, and prayers are answered just as we hoped. Other times, His yes is unexpected, appearing in ways we never imagined.

God's yes is always aligned with His will and purpose. He says yes when what we are asking aligns with His perfect plan, when it will bring Him glory, and when it will ultimately draw us closer to Him. Sometimes, His "yes" requires us to take a step of faith, to walk through a door even when we feel unprepared. Other times, it is a reminder that He delights in giving good gifts to His children.

Reflection Questions:

1. Think about a time when God answered your prayer with a yes. How did it impact your faith? Did it look the way you expected?
2. What prayers are you currently waiting on? How can you trust that God's answer—whether it is yes, no, or wait—is always for your good?

Conclusion:

No matter His answer, we can be confident that He hears us, loves us, and is always working for our ultimate good.

Final Thoughts

As we come to the end of this 30-day journey through God's "no," I want to take a moment to acknowledge how difficult this topic can be. It's never easy to face disappointment, especially when the answers we long for are not the ones we receive. But even in the midst of these moments, one thing remains true: God is faithful. His love and His plan for you never change, even when it feels like the door is closed.

I know some of you may be in a season where it feels like the answer is always "no." Maybe you're facing challenges, feeling overlooked, or wondering why God isn't answering your prayers the way you expect. I want to encourage you today to lean into the truth that God is for you. He is not against you. Even when it feels like He's saying "no," it's not a rejection of you, but a redirection towards something greater.

When we walk through tough times, it's natural to want to understand why. And let me assure you, it's okay to ask God questions. It's okay to feel confused, hurt, or even angry. Those feelings are part of the journey, and God is big enough to handle them. He welcomes your honesty and your heart. The key is to not let those feelings pull you away from Him, but to press in and trust that even when you don't understand, He is working on your behalf.

So, remember this: a "no" from God doesn't mean "never." Sometimes it simply means, "not yet," or "I have something better." Trust that His timing is perfect, even when it doesn't match yours.

As we close this devotional, I hope you leave knowing that you are not alone in this journey. God is with you, and He is always working behind the scenes for your good. My prayer is that this devotional has helped you reflect on your own faith, strengthen your trust in Him, and go deeper in your relationship with Jesus. You are loved, and you are never forgotten.

About The Author

In When God Says No, Eat Cake, I share my journey of navigating life's disappointments and discovering joy in the most unexpected places. With over 25 years of experience in corporate sales and coaching, I've witnessed firsthand the transformative power of embracing one's authentic self, even in the face of life's most difficult trials. My own path of self-discovery led me to become a certified Freedom Coach and Ramsey Financial Coach, allowing me to help others overcome limiting beliefs and confidently step into their calling and purpose. Through a holistic and biblical approach that integrates relationships, finances, and personal growth, I empower others to find fulfillment and success on their own terms. This book is a heartfelt reminder that God's "no" isn't the end of the story—it's an opportunity to find joy and blessings in unexpected places. And sometimes, it looks like simply enjoying a piece of cake.

LinkedIn: https://www.linkedin.com/in/rhonda-velez-414a7026/
Facebook: https://www.facebook.com/rhonda.velez
Instagram: https://www.instagram.com/realityoflife02/
Website: https://www.rhondavelez.com